My House Is Your House

Written by
Carmen Tafolla

Illustrated by
Gilles Eduar

Rigby.
A Harcourt Achieve Imprint

www.Rigby.com
1-800-531-5015

Grandma came from Mexico
and taught us many things.
She always said,
"When someone comes
to your door,
treat them well.
Smile at them,
ask them in,
and tell them
with a loving grin. . .

"My house is your house.
Mi casa es su casa."

A little girl
came to our door,
so lost and all alone.
Well, we didn't want her
to feel bad, so
we smiled at her,
asked her in,
and told her
with a loving grin. . .

4

"My house is your house.
Mi casa es su casa."

A tired old man
came to our door
with ten tired children, too.
Well, we didn't want them
to feel bad, so
we smiled at them,
asked them in,
and told them
with a loving grin. . .

"My house is your house.
Mi casa es su casa."

7

A scrawny cat
came to our door
with twenty scrawny kittens, too.
Well, we didn't want them
to feel bad, so
we smiled at them,
asked them in,
and told them
with a loving grin. . .

"My house is your house.
Mi casa es su casa."

An army of crickets
came to our door,
looking for a place to play.
Well, we didn't want them
to feel bad, so
we smiled at them,
asked them in,
and told them
with a loving grin. . .

"My house is your house.
Mi casa es su casa."

Then ten thousand termites
came to our wooden door,
looking for something to eat,
looking at our walls,
looking at our halls,
looking at our house of wood,
like no termite ever should.

Well, we didn't want them
to feel bad, so
we smiled at them. . .
but did not ask them in
and this time told them,
with a loving grin. . .

13

15